GOOD for NOTHIN' MEN!

by Carroll Zahn

CCC Publications

Published by

CCC Publications
9725 Lurline Avenue
Chatsworth, CA 91311

Manufactured in the United States of America.

Cover & interior art by Carroll Zahn.

Cover design by Carroll Zahn.

Cover production by Continental Imaging Center.

ISBN: 1-57644-122-9

If your local bookstore is out of stock, copies of this book may be obtained by mailing check or money order for $6.99 per book (plus $2.75 to cover postage and handling) to: CCC Publications, 9725 Lurline Avenue, Chatsworth, CA 91311.

Pre-publication Edition - 7/01

Dedicated to all the women
who have ever been in love
with a good for nothin' man.

Introduction

Good for nothin' men are two-timing, lying, cheating, foul-mouthed, filthy-minded slimeballs! They're dirty, rotten, smelly, unshaven bums who belch, fart and scratch their crotches and butts anywhere they feel like it! They love hot sex, cold booze, big boobs and boob tubes!

But no matter how obnoxius they are, they just don't get it!! Probably because they're arrogant, self-loving, macho, narrow-minded, chauvinist pigs!

...Other than that, they're not so bad.

In the BEGINNING...

"It's tails, Eve, you lose. You bear the children."

1.

All men think they're GREAT in bed!

2.

If only the good die young...Ed is going to live forever!

"I should have known my ex was a bum when his check for the marriage license bounced!"

there's no sports
on TV...want to
make love ?

Charlie is number 1!
...when it comes to BAD examples!
CHIPS
Zahn

Some men grow old gracefully...
Fred wasn't one of them!
BLAAT!

"You know you're the only woman in the world for me, Stella, expect for my wife, of course."

"I didn't say I wanted to pay you a compliment! I said how much would you pay me for a compliment?"

GOOD for NOTHIN' MEN number 2

HOSPITAL ADMINIS

"My woman is going to be here for a few days...could I get a loner?"

zahn

I'd like to toast a man of excellent taste...

If I only knew one!

"It's your wife, Al....are you here?"

GOOD for NOTHIN' MEN number 3

The weirdo who surfs the web for porno 12 hours a day!

"Don't move. I want something to remember you by.... after the divorce!"

"Being of sound mind I spent all my money on booze and broads."

"They tell me I'm going to have a conjugal visit and I get all excited. Then it turns out to be my wife!

"It's quite obvious to me, Mrs. Crawford, you're married to a total IDIOT!"

...but most men think they know too much anyhow!

GOOD for NOTHIN' MEN number 4

"The following program contains nudity and graphic violence and may be offensive to some viewers..."

"I've never been much of a do-it-yourself kind of a guy... could you give me a hand?"

"I must've got a bad olive at the bar last night."

"I'm complimenting you on your chili."

GOOD for NOTHIN' MEN number 5

The fat slob who thinks he looks and sings like Elvis!

"I'm watching this great show on 'pleasing your mate' and I don't want to miss any of it. After you put the groceries away, bring me another beer."

"Other than my fantastic good looks and extraordinary humility, what else was it that attracted you to me?"

Some men are
real crack-ups!
Zahn

"Well, I'll be... I caught a fish!"

"I'll take out the garbage as soon as football season is over!"

GOOD for NOTHIN' MEN number 6

"You really should give me a little credit, not many men could cope with failure the way I have."

"When I got hit by that truck last week, my whole life FLASHED before my eyes!"

"No, I'm sorry, my wife's not here right now."

Me and my woman had a beautiful relationship and then she began defending herself!"

"I'm trying to quit smoking. Would you mind if I use one of those as a pacifier?"

Ralph is multi-talented. He can belch, scratch, fart and change the TV channel all at the same time.

"From now on I won't miss any important plays in a game!"

GOOD for NOTHIN' MEN number 7

The guy who is OLD, FAT and UGLY and still thinks he's GOD'S gift to women!

"It's a love-hate relationship. I love the woman... my wife hates her!"

"You must know I'm serious about those...er...us."

" You know my world revolves around you, Honey, except during baseball, football and basketball season! "

"I think that broad has the hots for us... she's checking out our butts."

Couch potatoes have a certain magnetism about them....
not animal..VEGETABLE!

GOOD for NOTHIN' MEN number 8

The REAL jerk-off!

Jerry knew if he wanted to be a sexual athlete he had to practice, practice, practice!

"You're going to meet a tall, dark,
handsome and good for nothing man!"

JOE POTATO

"My woman asked me what I'd do if I ran out of BEER and there was no SPORTS on TV. I told her we'd have SEX!"

"It's Jerry's idea of humor."

GOOD for NOTHIN' MEN number 9

The Romantic Old Fart

LOVE is in the air!

"You should have known better then to smoke in bed with an inflatable doll!"

Before I met Tony
I thought SEX
was dirty!

Now I know it is!

"He doesn't drink coffee because he thinks it makes him hyper active."

SO HOW WAS YOUR **BLIND DATE** LAST NIGHT, DONNA?
O B WHEELER

BLIND DRUNK!
Zahn

"I wish I was fooling around on my wife half as much as she thinks I am!"

GOOD for NOTHIN' MEN number 10

The fat, beer guzzling, junk food junkie!

"Please excuse Steve... he hates pretentiousness!"

"I might run out of beer before this storm is over, Babe, you better go out and get some more!"

Otto needed a convenient spot to set his beer on, so Helga gave him a belly button ring with a coaster attachment!
?
Zahn

IN CASE OF HARASSMENT
BREAK GLASS
MACE

"Make up your mind! First you tell me I'm watching too much sports and now you say I'm watching too much porno!"

The danger of what can happen to a woman who has a long-term relationship with a good for nothin' man!

"I must have really had a great time last night! I've already puked four times!"

GOOD for NOTHIN' MEN number 11

"Helen! I'm all settled in and I don't want to get up. Would you get the TV remote for me?"

"My boyfriend was faithful until he hit the 'PEANUT SYNDROME'.. you know, he can't have just one!"

My marriage has
been a great success.
...I've managed to
eliminate many of my
my husbands disgusting
habits!

GOOD for NOTHIN' MEN number 12

"If you like oral sex, press 4... if you like kinky sex, press 5... if you like..."

"He scores! He scores again! This is a great porno video!"

"He didn't ask me to swallow my pride,
he asked me to swallow his pride!"

"How many shots did you have at the 19th hole?"

KET
5 $159
I'VE GOT VIAGRA!
I'VE GOT A HEADACHE!
Zahn

When you fall for a
good for nothin' man
you may be left
holding the bag!

GOOD for NOTHIN' MEN number 13

The Cigarettes and Whiskey and Wild, Wild Women Man!

"I DRINK, SMOKE and CHEAT so I'll have something to give up when my health starts to go!"

TITLES BY CCC PUBLICATIONS, LLC

PARTY / CARTOON BOOKS - Retail $4.99 - $6.99

101 SIGNS/SPENDING TOO MUCH TIME W/ CAT
ARE WE DYSFUNCTIONAL YET?
ARE YOU A SPORTS NUT?
BETTER HALF, The
BOOK OF WHITE TRASH, The
BUT OSSIFER, IT'S NOT MY FAULT
CAT OWNER'S SHAPE-UP MANUAL
CYBERGEEK IS CHIC
DIFFERENCE BETWEEN MEN & WOMEN, The
FITNESS FANATICS
FLYING FUNNIES
GOLFAHOLICS
GOOD FOR NOTHIN' MEN
GO TO HEALTH!
IF MEN HAD BABIES...
LOVE & MARRIAGE & DIVORCE
LOVE DAT CAT
MALE BASHING: WOMEN'S FAVORITE PASTIME
MARITAL BLISS & OTHER OXYMORONS
MORE THINGS YOU CAN DO WITH A USELESS MAN
OFFICE FROM HELL, The
OH BABY!
PMS CRAZED: TOUCH ME AND I'LL KILL YOU!
SLICK EXCUSES FOR STUPID SCREW-UPS
SMART COMEBACKS FOR STUPID QUESTIONS
SO, YOU'RE GETTING MARRIED
SO, YOU'RE HAVING A BABY
TECHNOLOGY BYTES!
THINGS/DO WITH/USELESS MAN "G-Rated"
THINGS YOU'LL NEVER HEAR THEM SAY
WHY GOD MAKES BALD GUYS
WHY MEN ARE CLUELESS
YOUR COMPUTER THINKS YOU'RE AN IDIOT

GAG / BLANK BOOKS - Retail $4.99 - $5.99

ALL/WAYS MEN/SMARTER THAN WOMEN (blank)
ALL/WAYS WOMEN/SMARTER THAN MEN (blank)
COMPLETE GUIDE/RETIREMENT'S GREAT ACTIVITIES
COMPLETE GUIDE TO SEX AFTER 30 (blank)
COMPLETE GUIDE TO SEX AFTER 40 (blank)
COMPLETE GUIDE TO SEX AFTER 50 (blank)
COMPLETE GUIDE TO SEX AFTER BABY (blank)
COMPLETE GUIDE TO SEX AFTER MARRIAGE (blank)
COMPLETE GUIDE TO OVER-THE-HILL SEX (blank)
LAST DIET BOOK, The (gag)

AGE RELATED / OVER THE HILL - Retail $4.99 - $6.99

30 - DEAL WITH IT
40 - DEAL WITH IT
50 - DEAL WITH IT
60 - DEAL WITH IT
OVER THE HILL - DEAL WITH IT!
CRINKLED & WRINKLED
RETIREMENT: THE GET EVEN YEARS
SENIOR CITIZEN'S SURVIVAL GUIDE, The
WELCOME TO YOUR MIDLIFE CRISIS
YIKES, IT'S ANOTHER BIRTHDAY
YOU KNOW YOU'RE AN OLD FART WHEN...
YOUNGER MEN ARE BETTER THAN RETIN-A

MINI BOOKS (4 x 6) Retail $4.99 - $6.99

"?" [question mark book]
IT'S A MAD MAD MAD SPORTS WORLD
LITTLE BOOK OF CORPORATE LIES, The
LITTLE BOOK OF ROMANTIC LIES, The
LITTLE INSTRUCTION BOOK OF RICH & FAMOUS
NOT TONIGHT DEAR, I HAVE A COMPUTER
OLD, FAT, WHITE GUY'S GUIDE TO EBONICS, The
SINGLE WOMEN vs. MARRIED WOMEN
TAKE A WOMAN'S WORD FOR IT

TRADE PAPERBACKS Retail $4.99 - $7.99

50 WAYS TO HUSTLE YOUR FRIENDS
1001 WAYS TO PROCRASTINATE
ABSOLUTE LAST CHANCE DIET BOOK
BOTTOM HALF, The
EVERYTHING I KNOW/LEARNED/TRASH TALK TV
GETTING OLD SUCKS!
GETTING EVEN W/ ANSWERING MACH
GREATEST ANSWERING MACHINE MESSAGES
HOW TO ENTERTAIN PEOPLE YOU HATE
HOW TO GET FREE FOOD IN COLLEGE
HOW TO REALLY PARTY!
HOW TO SURVIVE A JEWISH MOTHER
HOW TO TALK/WAY OUT OF/TRAFFIC TICKET
IT'S BETTER/OVER THE HILL THAN UNDER IT
I WISH I DIDN'T...
KILLER BRAS
LADIES, START YOUR ENGINES
LIFE'S MOST EMBARRASSING MOMENTS
HORMONES FROM HELL
HORMONES FROM HELL II
HUSBANDS FROM HELL
MEN LOVE FOOTBALL/WOMEN LOVE FOREPLAY
NEVER A DULL CARD
PEOPLE WATCHER'S FIELD GUIDE
RED HOT MONOGAMY
SHARING THE ROAD WITH IDIOTS
UGLY TRUTH ABOUT MEN
UNOFFICIAL WOMEN'S DIVORCE GUIDE
WHAT DO WE DO NOW?? (New Parents)
WHY MEN DON'T HAVE A CLUE
WORK SUCKS!

"ON THE EDGE" - Retail $4.99 - $6.99

ART OF MOONING, The
COMPLETE BOOGER BOOK, The
COMPLETE WIMP'S GUIDE TO SEX, The
FARTING
SEX AND YOUR STARS
SEX IS A GAME
SEXY CROSSWORD PUZZLES
SIGNS YOUR SEX LIFE IS DEAD
THE TOILET ZONE
THINGS/DO WITH/USELESS MAN "R-Rated"
TOTAL BASTARD'S GUIDE TO GOLF, The
YOU KNOW HE'S/WOMANIZING SLIMEBALL WHEN...